AMAZING IRONWORKERS
BUILDING NEAR YOU
BY STARR COBURN

SKYWALKERS

SKYSCRAPERS

IRONWORKERS CAN BUILD ANYTHING

BUILDING NEAR YOU

FACTORS

HOSPITALS

STADUIMS

AIRPORTS

This book is dedicated to all the amazing ironworkers from around the world.

Thank you for all your hard work.

Library of Congress Cataloging in Publication Data
The Cataloging in Publication Data for Amazing Ironworkers on file at the Library of Congress.
LCCN: 2020920879
ISBN: 978-1-7332183-8-2

Published in the United States of America by Starr Elite Publishing.
starrelitepublishing@gmail.com
Copy 2020 Starr Elite Publishing
All rights reserved. No part of this book may be reproduced or utilized in any form or by any means without written permission from the publisher.

Some photos by Maarten van den Heuvel, Dina karan, Nik Shuliahin, Belinda Fewings, AussieActive , Johnson liu, Koes Nadi, Jue Huang, Jue Huang, Sunyu Kim, sergio souza, Alex Haney, Matheron T Rader, David Martin, Tanya Nevidoma on Unsplash. Tom Fisk from Pexels.

Table of Contents

Amazing Ironworkers 4
Ironworker Tools 38
Fun Facts 39
About the Author 40

Meet some of the many amazing ironworkers who help build America.

Hugh Craig
Local 86

Kaylan Norberg
Local 24

Jonh Irwin
LOCAL 402

Chris Brown
Local 709

Kalena Firstrider
LOCAL 86

Marvin Duncan
Local 396

Cody McCoy
LOCAL 27

Robert Crump
Local 75

Ironworkers are awesome! They are brave, smart, strong, hard-working men and women.

Abbey Howes   LOCAL 103

Nathan Brooks   Local 1

Christopher Congdon Local 15

Those who want to be an ironworker must attend vocational school for three or four years. As an apprentice ironworker, they are taught everything they need to know to become a journeyman ironworker also known as boomer.

Chelsey Sorensen Local 397

Lee Blancarte Local 378

Ironworkers adhere to safety rules and regulations by wearing tool belts to hold their tools, hard hats to protect their head and safety glasses to protect their eyes.

Stuart Brooks — Local 387

Joshua Cruz — LOCAL 378

Bill Masters — Local 8

Ironworkers are universal.

Rocky Lafontaine   LOCAL 720

Shannon Russell   LOCAL 433

William Colern   LOCAL 6

Not only do they build in the state where they live, but some travel around the world to help with building projects.

Matt Wimer — Local 549

Louis Bellegarde — Local 771

Paul Flores — Local 229

T'Ina Pete
Local 720

Caleb Ellison
LOCAL 92

Tim Ware
Local 10

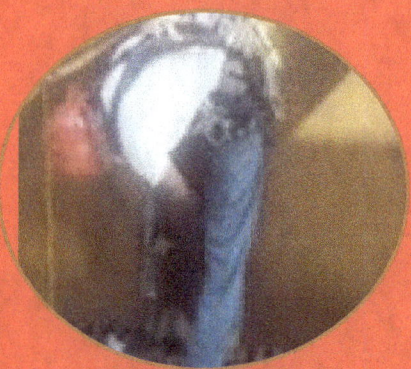
Tim Charles
LOCAL 782

Kevin Bean
LOCAL 48

Louis Bellegarde
Local 771

Dylan Doane
Local 771

Chris Gray

Brad Hutchelson
Local 103

Anthony Trovato
LOCAL 21

Luke Mauro
LOCAL 21

Ironworkers are courageous and perform great balancing acts while working.

James Loiudice — LOCAL 361

Eron Martin — Local 29

Anthony Ivaldi — Local 377

They work underground and high in the sky.

Barrett Lewis   LOCAL 118

Brad Toland   LOCAL 86

Travis Camacho   Local 580

Josh Dyke   Local 147

Ryan Beecham   Local 728

Jason Dubowsky   Local 15

For extra safety ironworkers wear a harness to keep them secure while they are working six feet and higher aboveground.

Clyde Alderson - Local 5

James Arsenault Local 721

Patrick Anicito   Local 70

Don Stoddard
Local 3

Barry Jheeta
Local 720

Pete Buccellato
Local 25

Owewn Murray
Local 7

Andrew Larsen
LOCAL 10

Tommy Jock jr.
Local 440

John Sinnes
Local 380

Zaira Trovato
LOCAL 21

Jason Lopez
Local 397

They provide quality workmanship in welding steel together and connecting bolts to prevent construction mishap.

Lawrence Green - LOCAL 433

Korey - Local 63

Eve Pearson LOCAL 798

Ironworkers work all year round: spring, summer, winter, and fall. They work when it's hot. They work when it's cold. They even work when it snows.

Cody Mitchell - LOCAL 89

Tara Wayne - LOCAL 86

Kasey Clouse - Local 112

They work long hours. Some work during the day. Some work at night.

Alexander Reyes LOCAL 229

Daniel Ioerger Local 112

Depodray Coburn Local 387

Brain Balderstone
LOCAL 728

Floyd Denny
Local 433

Eve Pearson & Her Son J.C. Flowers

Daniel Ditimus
Local 387

Cody Mitchell
Local 89

Crystal Doolittle
Local 720

Jason Nacey
Local 24

Nicolas Morin
Local 711

Steve Aycock
Local 597

There are three types of ironworkers: reinforcing, structural and ornamental.

Caleb Ellison   LOCAL 92

Nick Bryan
Local 10

Collin Werths
Local 10

Katrina Jones   LOCAL 721

Reinforcing ironworkers are sometimes called rodbusters.

They are responsible for installing steel bars on the ground or on a wall.

This prevents the buildings and roads from collapsing.

Billy Clyburn — LOCAL 290

Jesse McKnight — LOCAL 383

Jennifer Santos — Local 711

Charles Poole
LOCAL 395

Raymond Abrams
Local 397

Cody Spears
Local 263

Erin Goggins
Local 751

Ron Ware Sr.
LOCAL 10

Michael Johnson
Local 92

Cody Hannah
Local 492

Jesse Flores
LOCAL 433

Hunter Barber
Local 397

Structural ironworkers assemble the framework of the project they build.

They erect cranes and other big machines needed to complete the projects.

Brad Kirk   LOCAL 97   Shawn Garrels LOCAL 97

Rayna Lorraine   LOCAL 86

Alexander Reyes   Local 229

Chris Vazquez   Local 84   Chad M. Wildman   Local 25

Ornamental ironworkers are the last on the job.

They install windows, handrails, metal stairways, gates and lamp posts.

Richard Shirah Local 387

Timothy Collins Local 7

Chealse Smith   Local 495

Ironworkers build a broad spectrum of buildings such as...

Vania Adina   Local 155

Dre Coburn   Juana Durana
Local 387   Local 433

Tyler Day   Curtis Wilcox
Local 732   Local 387

Tricia Sparvier   Local 721

Kelvin K. Woods   Local 167

Joshua Dyke   Local 147

hospitals people visit when they are not feeling well:

factories that make, food, cars, and material we need:

tall buildings called skyscrapers where people live and work:

schools you attend to learn and play with friends:

airports that gives us access to airplanes.

They install towers that gives us internet and phone signals.

Henry Rodriguez

They assemble the roller coasters we love to ride and the slides we enjoy when we go to amusement parks or carnivals.

Zachary Irvine   Local 808

Anthony Viviani   Local 11

Michael Taylor
Local 433

Harley Thompson
Local 397

Arlo Wanatee
Local 67

Corie Slaughter
Local 623

Ohitikahwin Beautiful Bald Eagle
Local 433

Shondez George
Local 7

Ray Curry
Local 395

John Pidgeon
LOCAL 420

Steve Smith
Local 397

Ironworkers assemble wind turbines to obtain electricity which powers thousands of homes and businesses.

Susan is working 240 feet in the air.

Susan Mann   Local 433

Local 842   New Brunswick

Chris Schaefer
Local 395

Gabe Flores
LOCAL 229

Mark Raber Jr.
Local 263

Jordan Heer
LOCAL 732

Jamie Behn
Local 111

Scott Fadden
Local 11

Charles Robbins
Local 378

Marc Green
LOCAL 8

Linda Landin
LOCAL 482

Ironworkers also build sports stadiums, grocery stores, mega churches and department stores.

Travis Wellard   Local 732

The unique design of the Golden Gate Bridge in California, Sunshine Bridge in Florida, Brooklyn Bridge in New York, and others were constructed by ironworkers.

Lee Farley — LOCAL 9
Bridget Booker - LOCAL 112
Jake Swartz — LOCAL 444

Ironworkers had the privilege of working on the Gateway Arch located in Saint Louis, Missouri and repairing the Statue of Liberty located on Ellis Island in New York.

Branden Hardy
Local 292

Jonathan Marriott
LOCAL 752

Ron Ware Sr.
Local 10

Josh Geyer
Local 97

Jaycob Moore
LOCAL 48

Cody Moore
LOCAL 395

Annie Martin
Local 29

Jasmine Penny
Local 392

Vicent Dozier
LOCAL 58

A ceremony is held when the ironworkers sign their name on the last beam to be raised and put in place to finish the project.

The quality of the material and the professional workmanship of the ironworkers ensure that the build will last for many years.

Patti Kreitner - Local 11

Topping out Ceremony

Lawrence Greene Local 433

Ironworker signing their name on the last beam.

Jason Brock Local 25   Shane Brock Local 25

Alex Flores
LOCAL 512

Paul Flores
LOCAL 229

Gabe Flores
LOCAL 229

David Blanks   Trent Risner   Don Stoddard

Can you imagine how the world would look without ironworkers.

If you were an ironworker what would you build?

Fun Fact:

One World Trade Center located in New York city is the tallest building in America.

It's 1,776 feet tall and 1,792 feet tall if you measure from the ground to the tip of the building.

It has 94 floors.

Meet the Author

Starr is an outgoing, free spirited individual. Since childhood she always dreamed of writing books. A native of St. louis, Missouri currently living in New Jersey, she is married and has three amazing boys. Her published books include: Jojo the Amazing Ironworker, Amazing Ironworkers Coloring book and There Goes the Barber.
Connect with her at:
www.starr-coburn.com
Facebook: Author Starr Coburn
Instagram: author_sic

www.ingramcontent.com/pod-product-compliance
Lightning Source LLC
Chambersburg PA
CBHW081410070526
44583CB00020B/2752